2nd EDITION
INCREDIBLE ENGLISH

GW01090399

Class Book

2

Sarah Phillips

Kirstie Grainger   Michaela Morgan   Mary Slattery

OXFORD
UNIVERSITY PRESS

Language summary

1 New friends

What day is it today?
Who's that? That's …
She's my (sister).
He's my (brother).
How old is he / she?
He's / She's (8).

Days of the week: Monday Tuesday Wednesday Thursday Friday Saturday Sunday
Characters: Flo Fred Bing Titch Poppy Mr Fixit Norton Mitch
Numbers: 13–30
Measuring: metre centimetre
Other: sunny

2 The treehouse

Is he / she / it in / on / under the table?
He's / She's / It's in / on / under the …

Furniture: bed cupboard table box chair shelf cushion sofa rug
House: window picure mirror vase door
Other: treehouse hamster cage

3 Come and play!

He's / She's got a …

Toys: scooter kite skateboard skipping rope yo-yo boat frisbee ball bat bike
Transport: lorry helicopter plane motorbike van wheel
Other: broken skip tricks

4 At the wildlife park

It can … / It can't …
Can it …? / Yes / No
Can you guess …?
(Walk) like a (penguin).

Wild animals: dolphin bat zebra crocodile snake parrot penguin monkey lion giraffe
Parts of an animal: wings tail beak feathers
Other: stretch slide climb jump run play a game fly thank you juggle

5 At the shop

Can I have … please?
Yes, here you are.
No, sorry.
Plural nouns
How much …?
Can he / she buy …?

Small toys: sharpeners rubbers stickers marbles balloons badges dinosaurs key rings felt tips figures
Numbers: 31–100
Money: pound p
Other: paper string surprise coin

6 Lunchtime

Do you like …?
What's your favourite …?
Do you want …?

Food: cheese tuna chicken tomatoes sardines sausages rice bread lettuce eggs
Food groups: meat fish dairy fruit vegetables cereal
Other: sandwich lunch salad white bread brown bread

7 At the fair

Are you …?
Yes. / No, I'm …
I feel …
What's the matter?
What can you hear?

Feelings: sad happy scared cross bored sleepy dizzy hungry thirsty hot cold
Musical instruments: violin piano flute xylophone guitar
Other: fair great fantastic brilliant hot dog ride zoo

8 At home

What are you doing?
I'm …ing.
I'm / He's / She's busy.
Go away.
It's raining.
How much water?
I / You need …

Indoor activities: watch TV read play on the computer do my homework cook make a model paint sleep do a puzzle
Uses of water: wash my hands have a shower wash up clean my teeth have a bath litre
Other: hole bottle hop

9 At the pool

What's he / she doing?
He's / She's …ing.
Look at me.
Over there.

Outdoor activities: swim float write a postcard eat an ice cream drink a milkshake read a comic listen to the radio watch have a shower take a photo
Children's games: play leapfrog play marbles dance play with a top
Other: smile pool fountain sun summer beach river spinner spin fingers feet

1 New friends

1 Listen and say who. 🔊 1.1
2 Listen and sing. 🔊 1.2

Norton

Mr Fixit

Day	Monitors	
	🪴	🐹
Monday	Flo	Fred
Tuesday	Poppy	Bing
Wednesday	Titch	Flo
Thursday	Flo	Bing
Friday	Fred	Titch
Saturday		Poppy
Sunday		Poppy

Poppy

Bing

Titch

Fred

Flo

1 Listen and point. 1.5

Let's make friends!

2 Find and number. Say.

3 Listen again and act. 1.5

1 Listen, count and find. 1.6
Say the letters.

How old is he? He's 8.

How old is she? She's 11.

2 Listen and follow. What colour is the door? 1.7

  8  7  6  9

  7  6  9  8

  6  9  8  10

  9  8  10  8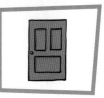

1 Listen and sing. 🎵 1.10

Hello, what's your name?
Hello, come and play!
Hello, don't be shy!
Come and be my friend!

Measuring

1 **Listen and chant.** 🔊 1.11
2 **Read and say who.**

30 —
29 — Martin
28 —
27 —
26 —
25 —
24 —
23 —
22 —
21 — Max
20 —
19 —
18 —
17 —
16 —
15 —
14 — Nicola
13 —
12 —
11 —
10 —
9 —
8 — Becky
7 —
6 —
5 —
4 —
3 —
2 —
1 —

1 metre

> I'm 1 metre 14 centimetres.

1

> I'm 1 metre 8 centimetres.

2

I'm 1 metre 29 centimetres.

I'm 1 metre 21 centimetres.

3

4

1 Make a number game.

Colour.

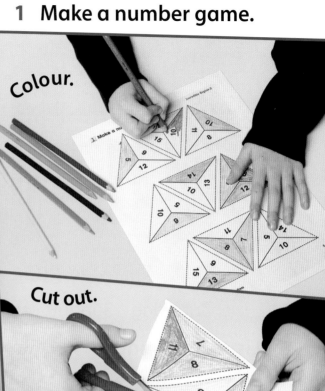

Cut out.

Play.

Take turns.

1 Listen and point. 🎧 1.13 **Listen again and repeat.**

Saturday   Sunday   sunny   Fran   Friday

2 Listen and match. 🎧 1.14 **Act out the dialogues.**

Who's that?   That's my friend, Tom.

How old is he?   He's eight.

Amy   9

Rob   7

Tom   8

2 | The treehouse

1 Listen and find. 🎧 1.17
2 Listen and sing. 🎧 1.18

box

sofa

cushion

table

cupboard

shelf

chair

rug

bed

1 Listen and point. 🔊 1.20

Hamster hide and seek

2 Find and number. Say.

3 Listen again and act. 1.20

1 Listen, find and say the numbers. 🎵 1.21

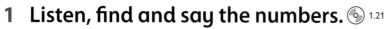

Is he in the cupboard?
Yes.

2 Listen and draw a line. 🎵 1.22

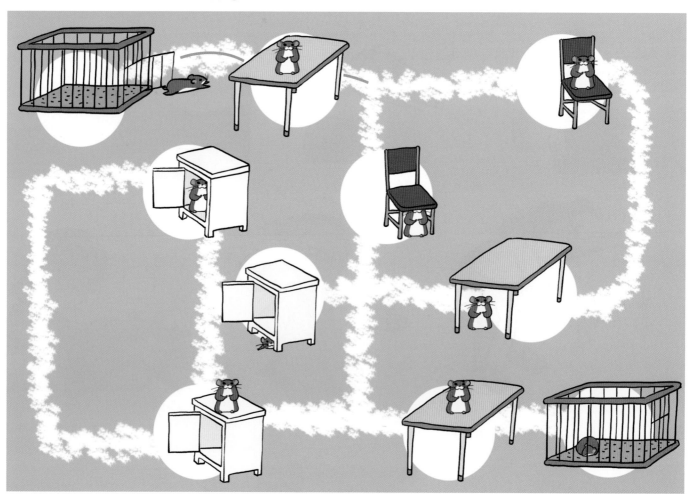

Lesson 5 ➡ AB pages 14–15

Is he in / on / under ...?

1 Listen and chant. 🔊 1.24

Song

Big books, small books,
Books on the shelf!
Books are fun,
Books can help!

Rooms in art

1 Listen, find and say. 🎵 1.25

mirror

door

picture

The Bedroom
Vincent Van Gogh

Room in Brooklyn
Edward Hopper

window

vase

table

3

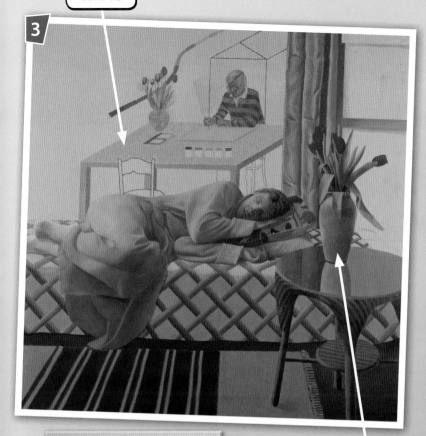

Model with unfinished self-portrait copyright David Hockney

vase

2 Read, look and find the mistakes.

Picture 1: The room is blue. It's got a black window. It's got a bed and a small table. It's got 6 pictures.

Picture 2: It's got a small table. It's got a vase. It's got a mirror.

Picture 3: It's got a bed. It's got a rug. It's got 3 vases. It's got a big table and a small table.

1 Make a collage.

Choose and colour.

Cut out.

Stick.

Write.

1 Listen and point. 🎧 1.26 Listen again and repeat.

two   toys   table

boy   bed   box

2 Play, ask and answer.

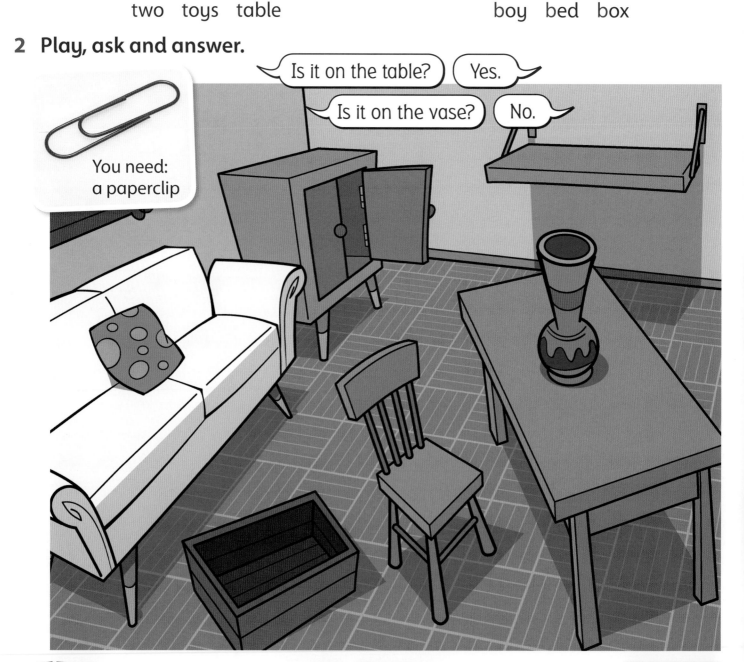

3 Come and play!

1 **Listen and find.** 🔘 1.28
2 **Listen and sing.** 🔘 1.29

boat

skipping rope

bike

scooter

kite

skateboard

yo-yo

ball

frisbee

bat

1 Listen and point. 1.31

2 Find and number. Say.

3 Listen again and act. 🔘 1.31

1 **Listen, find and say who.** 🎧 1.32

She's got a bike.

He's got a skateboard.

2 **Listen and say** *True* **or** *False.* 🎧 1.33

1 Listen and chant. 🔘 1.35

Song

I like skipping,
1, 2, 3!
I want Lucy
In with me!

L-U-C-Y

Goodbye, Lucy,
Wave at me!
Goodbye, Lucy,
1, 2, 3!

Venn diagrams

1 Listen and find. 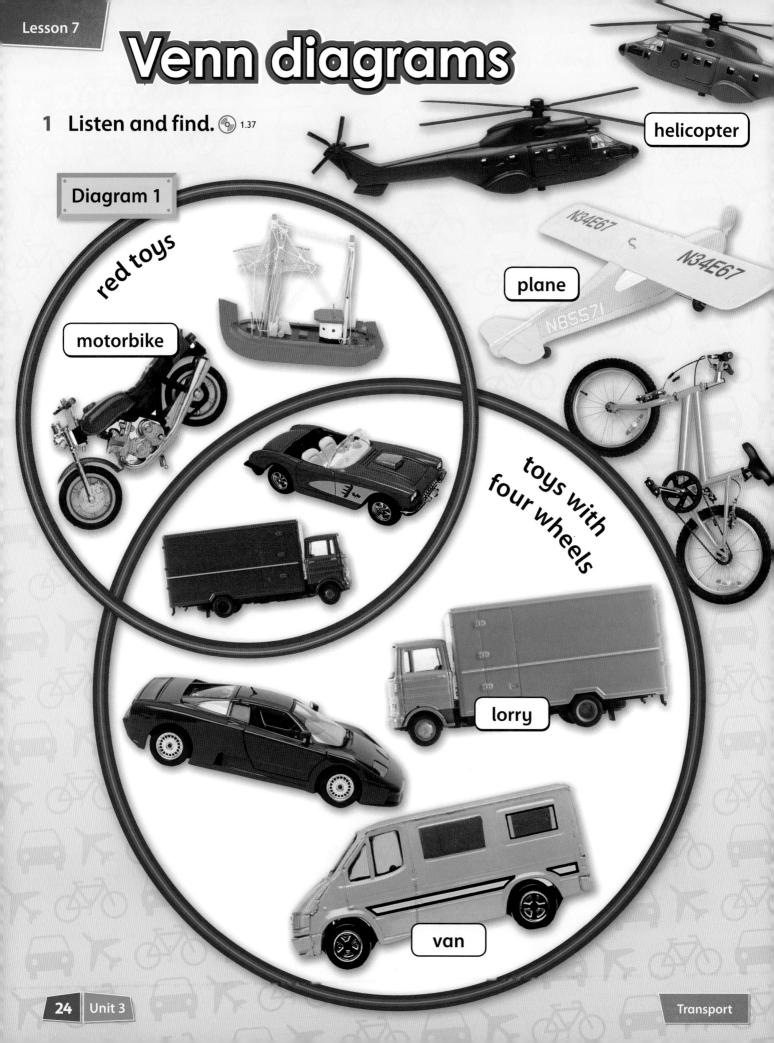 1.37

helicopter

Diagram 1

red toys

motorbike

plane

toys with four wheels

lorry

van

Diagram 2

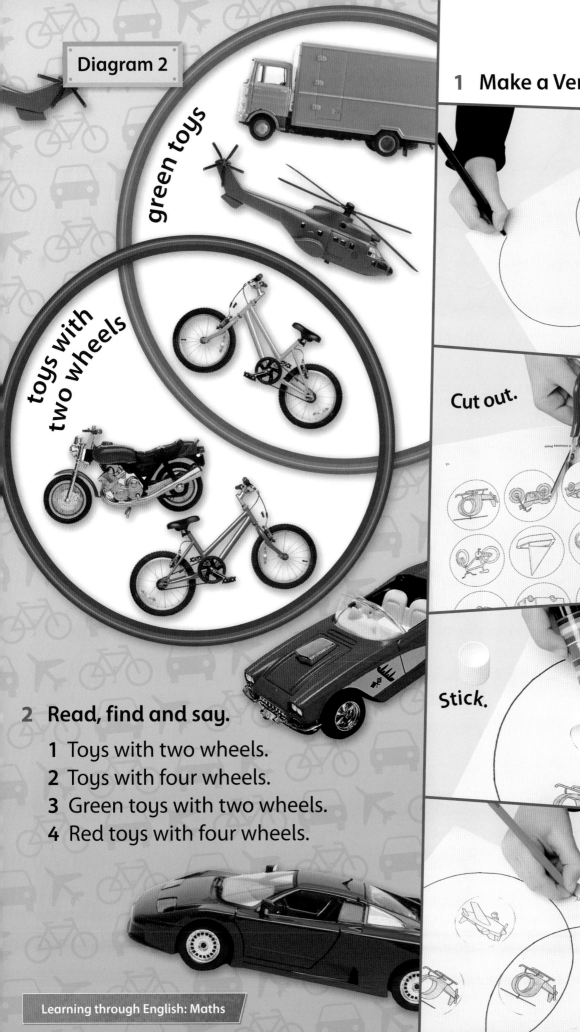

green toys

toys with two wheels

2 Read, find and say.

1 Toys with two wheels.
2 Toys with four wheels.
3 Green toys with two wheels.
4 Red toys with four wheels.

1 Make a Venn diagram.

Draw.

Cut out.

Stick.

Write.

1 Listen and point. 🔘 1.38 **Listen again and repeat.**

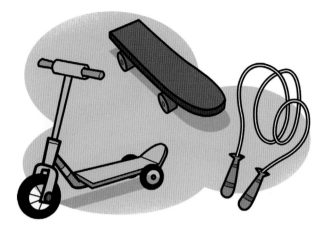

white   windows   wheels   scooter   skateboard   skipping rope

2 Listen, find and say the numbers. 🔘 1.39
Now it's your turn.

He's got a kite. She's got a skateboard.

I know! Number 2.

Me and my world

1 Read and number.

2 Read again, listen and check. 🔘 1.41

wall

floor

3 This is my *sister's bedroom*. She's got lots of toys in the box and on the floor and on her bed! Her favourite toy is a yo-yo. She's got 25 yo-yos!

Hello! I'm Nkoyo. I'm from Nigeria. I'm eight. These are my friends Asa and Ivie. They're eight too.

Hi! I'm Megan. I'm from Wales. I'm nine. This is my sister. She's seven.

This is my *bedroom*. I share my room with my brother. It's got two beds and a *big cupboard*. It's got a blue and red rug on the floor. My brother loves football. He's got pictures of football players on the wall.

Start

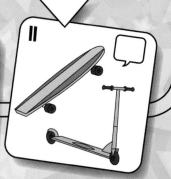

Finish

4 At the wildlife park

1 Listen and find. 2.1
2 Listen and chant. 2.2

zebra

giraffe

lion

monkey

snake

parrot

bat

crocodile

dolphin

penguin

1 Listen and point. 2.4

At the wildlife park

2 Find and number. Say.

3 Listen again and act. 2.4

1 Listen, find and say which animal. 🎧 2.5

It can swim.
It can't fly.
Can it run?

swim ✔
climb a tree ✘
run ✔
fly ✘

swim ✔
climb a tree ✔
run ✘
fly ✘

swim ✔
climb a tree ✘
run ✘
fly ✔

2 Listen and say *Parrot* or *Penguin*. Listen and repeat. 🎧 2.6–2.7

'Hello'

Lesson 5 ➤ AB pages 35–36

It can / can't ... Can it ...?

1 Listen and sing. 🔊 2.10

Song

The monkey says
'Now all watch me.'
The monkey says
'Look carefully.'
Can you do this?
Can you do this?
I can,
I can't,
And that's OK.
I can,
I can't,
We all can play!

Drawing

1 Listen and find. 2.11

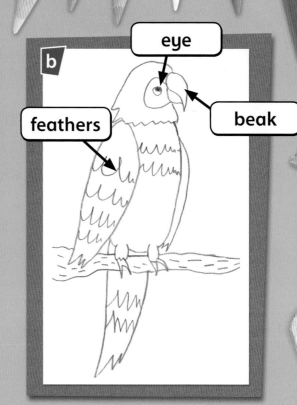

eye

feathers

beak

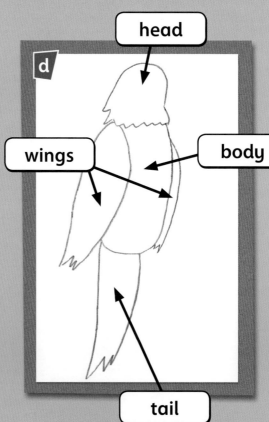

head

wings

body

tail

Parts of an animal

1 **Draw a penguin.**

Draw the head and body.

Draw the wings, eyes, beak and feet.

Colour.

Write.

2 **Read and find.**

1 My parrot has got a green tail and red wings.

2 My parrot has got yellow wings and a green head.

3 My parrot has got a red head and an orange beak.

4 My parrot has got a purple tail and a yellow beak.

1 Listen and point. 🔊 2.12 **Listen again and repeat.**

parrot   penguin   picture   orange   giraffe   juggle   jump

2 Listen and follow. 🔊 2.13 **Now it's your turn.**

(It can swim.)─(It's got a tail.)─(It's grey and white.)   (I know! It's a dolphin!)

5 At the shop

1 **Listen and find.** 🎧 2.15
2 **Listen and sing.** 🎧 2.16

dinosaurs

figures

sharpeners

rubbers

felt tips

balloons

marbles

key rings

badges

stickers

1 Listen and point. 2.18

The surprise

2 Find and number. Say.

3 Listen again and act. 2.18

1 Listen, find and say who. 2.19

> Can I have two figures, please?
> Here you are. / No, sorry.

2 Listen and say *Here you are* or *No, sorry*. 2.20

1 Listen and sing. 🔊 2.22

Let's make a card for Mum.

Yes, OK!

Let's make a card for Mum.

Yes, OK!

Let's make a card and say

'Hope you have a happy day'.

Let's make a card for Mum.

Yes, OK!

Caring for family and friends

Money

1 Listen and find. 🔊 2.23

£2 (pounds)

£1 (pound)

50p

20p

10p

5p

2p

1p

2 Read and say *Yes* or *No*.

50p

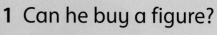

50p

60p

1 Can he buy a figure?

2 Can she buy a badge?

90p

80p

3 Can he buy stickers?

4 Can she buy a sharpener?

5 Can he buy a key ring?

1 Make some coins.

Colour.

Cut out.

Play shops.

Take turns.

1 Listen and point. 2.25 **Listen again and repeat.**

30p

thirty   thank you

mum   marble   motorbike

2 Listen, find and say how much. 2.26 **Act out the dialogues.**

Can I have three badges, please?   Here you are.

How much?   £1.50, please.

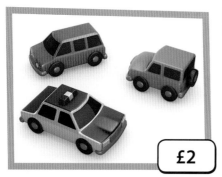

£2

30p

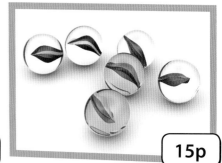

15p

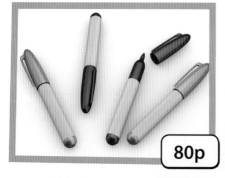

80p

50p

70p

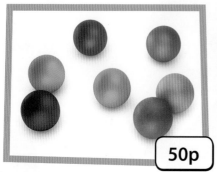

50p

30p

£1

6 Lunchtime

1 **Listen and find.** 🔊 2.28
2 **Listen and sing.** 🔊 2.29

bread

lettuce

tuna

cheese

sardines

tomatoes

sausages

rice

chicken

eggs

1 Listen and point. 🎧 2.31

Let's go fishing!

1 I've got lots of things in the kit today!

Oh. I've got a fish. It's big ... it's ...

2 ... a shoe!

Never mind. Let's have the sandwiches now. Do you want a cheese sandwich?

3 No, thank you. I don't like cheese.

I like cheese.

Egg for me, please!

4 I like cheese, I like eggs, I like lettuce, On brown bread.

5 Oh, no! It's a wheel!

Never mind, Mr Fixit. Do you want a cheese sandwich?

Yes please, Mitch.

6 Here you are. Oh, no!

2 Find and number. Say.

3 Listen again and act. 2.31

1 **Listen and find.** 🔊 2.32

2 **Listen and say how much.** 🔊 2.33

Do you like cheese?
Yes. / No.

3 **Listen, find and number.** 🔊 2.34

1 Listen and sing. 🎵 2.36

Song

Eggs and cheese for lunch today,
Eggs and cheese for lunch today,
Eggs and cheese for lunch today,
I'm trying something new today!

Trying different foods

Food

1 Listen, find and say. 🔊 2.38

From an animal

Fish

Meat

Dairy

From a plant

Cereal

Fruit

Vegetables

Food groups

2 Read and find.

1 My meal has got meat and vegetables.
2 My meal has got fish, vegetables and fruit.
3 My meal has got fruit and dairy.
4 My meal has got cereal, vegetables and dairy.

1 Make a food collage.

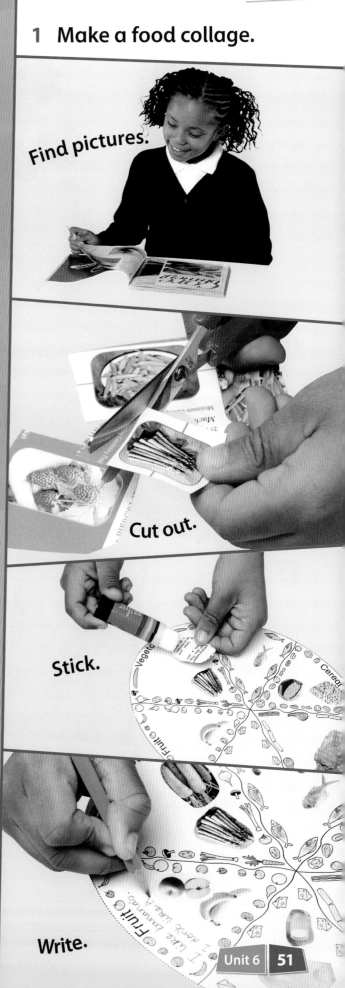

Find pictures.

Cut out.

Stick.

Write.

1 Listen and point. 🔊 2.39 Listen again and repeat.

cheese chicken chocolate   I've van vegetables

2 Listen and find. 🔊 2.40 Ask and answer.

Do you like bananas?

Yes.

No.

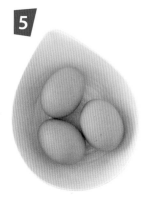

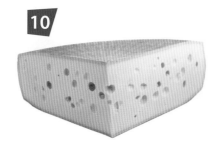

Me and my world

1 Read and number.

2 Read again, listen and check. 🔊 2.42

coconut milk

flour

rice

4 Blinis are traditional Russian food. They're small pancakes. Blinis are made from flour, milk and eggs.

☐ My name's Sergei. I'm from Russia. Blinis are my favourite food. On my birthday, I eat blinis with fruit and jam. They're delicious!

☐ Nasi lemak is traditional Malaysian food. It's made with rice and coconut milk.

☐ I'm Nurul. I live in Malaysia. My mum makes delicious nasi lemak. I like it with chicken, eggs and cucumber.

Start

Finish

7 At the fair

1 **Listen and find.** 🎧 2.44
2 **Listen and chant.** 🎧 2.45

scared

cold

hungry

hot

bored

thirsty

cross

sad

sleepy

dizzy

happy

1 Listen and point. 🔘 2.47

At the fair

1
I love fairs.
Me, too.
Do you like fairs, Mitch?
No.

2
Music, hot dogs,
Rides and fun.
Something here
For everyone!

3
This is great!
I'm dizzy. I don't like this.

4
Are you hungry?
Are you thirsty?
No. I don't like fairs.

5
Wow! It's fantastic!
Ooh, brilliant!
Oh, no. I'm scared! I don't like this!

2 Find and number. Say.

3 Listen again and act. 🔊 2.47

1 **Listen, find and say who. Listen and repeat.** 2.48–2.49

Are you sleepy?
Yes. / No.

Is he scared? Yes. / No.
Is she hungry? Yes. / No.

2 **Look at activity 1. Listen and answer.** 2.50

1 Listen and sing. 🎵 2.52

Smile at me when I feel sad,

I feel sad,

I feel sad.

Smile at me when I feel sad,

Now I feel better.

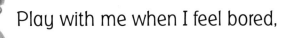

Play with me when I feel bored,

Talk to me when I feel cross,

Hold my hand when I feel scared,

Music

1 Listen, find and say.  2.54

1 violin

2 guitar

3 piano

4 flute

5 xylophone

Musical instruments

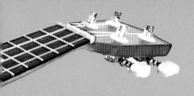

2 Read, listen and find. 🔘 2.55

1 I can hear a piano. When I hear this music, I feel sleepy.

2 I can hear a flute. When I hear this music, I feel dizzy.

3 I can hear a guitar. When I hear this music, I feel sad.

4 I can hear a xylophone. When I hear this music, I feel happy.

5 I can hear a violin. When I hear this music, I feel scared.

1 Draw a picture.

Listen.

Draw.

Colour.

Write.

Learning through English: Music

1 **Listen and point.** 🔊 3.2 **Listen again and repeat.**

hungry   hot   happy   dizzy   zebra   zoo

2 **Listen and number.** 🔊 3.3 **Act out the dialogues.**

Are you sleepy?

No, I'm hungry.

Here you are. Eat this.

Thanks.

Here you are. Drink this.

Here you are. Read this.

8 / At home

1 Listen and find. 🎧 3.5

2 Listen and chant. 🎧 3.6

make a model

sleep

read

do my homework

play on the computer

paint

cook

do a puzzle

watch TV

1 Listen and point. 3.8

Norton to the rescue!

2 Find and number. Say.

3 Listen again and act. 🎧 3.8

1 Listen, find and say who. 3.9

What are you doing?
I'm reading.

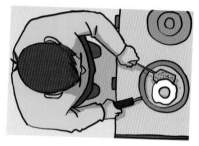

2 Listen and follow. What colour is the house? 3.10

    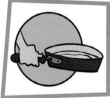 

1 Listen and sing. 🎵 3.12

Song

Oh, I'm lying on the sofa.
I'm sitting in the sun.
I'm bored of doing nothing.
Let's go out and have some fun!

Uses of water

This bottle has got 1 litre of water.

1 Listen, find and say. 🔊 3.13

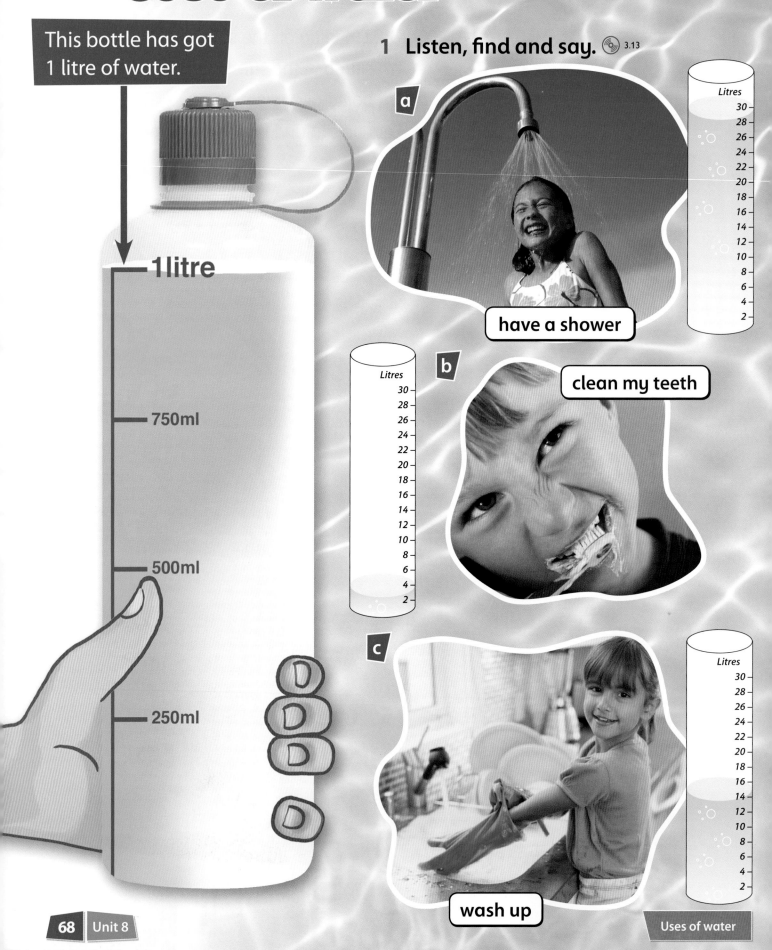

1litre

750ml

500ml

250ml

a

Litres
30
28
26
24
22
20
18
16
14
12
10
8
6
4
2

have a shower

clean my teeth

b

Litres
30
28
26
24
22
20
18
16
14
12
10
8
6
4
2

c

Litres
30
28
26
24
22
20
18
16
14
12
10
8
6
4
2

wash up

d have a bath

e

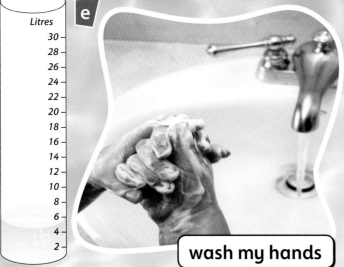

wash my hands

2 Read, look and say.

What are you doing?

1 You need 4 litres of water.

2 You need 30 litres of water.

3 You need 90 litres of water.

4 You need 6 litres of water.

5 You need 15 litres of water.

1 Make a water meter.

Tick.

Add.

Colour.

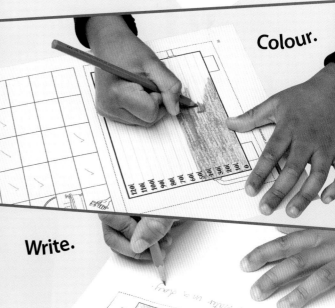

Write.

1 Listen and point. 🔊 3.15 **Listen again and repeat.**

wash   walk   watch

write   read   run

2 Listen and find. 🔊 3.16 **Mime, ask and answer.**

What are you doing?

I'm painting.

Lesson 10 ➔ AB pages 78–79

Speaking

9 At the pool

1 **Listen and find.** 🔘 3.18
2 **Listen and sing.** 🔘 3.19

take a photo

read a comic

write a postcard

eat an ice cream

listen to the radio

have a shower

watch

drink a milkshake

float

swim

1 Listen and point. 3.21

2 Find and number. Say.

3 Listen again and act. 🔘 3.21

1 **Listen and find.** 🎧 3.22

What's he doing? He's taking a photo.
What's she doing? She's swimming.

2 **Look at activity 1. Listen and say** *True* **or** *False*. 🎧 3.23

Lesson 5 ➤ AB pages 83–84

What's he / she doing? He's / She's ...ing.

1 Listen and sing. 🎧 3.25

Song

Summer's here,
Let's play in the sun.
We can swim, we can float,
We can jump, we can run.
But the sun is hot,
So remember the rules,
In the garden, at the beach and
  the swimming pool!

Children's games in art

1 Listen and find. 🎧 3.26

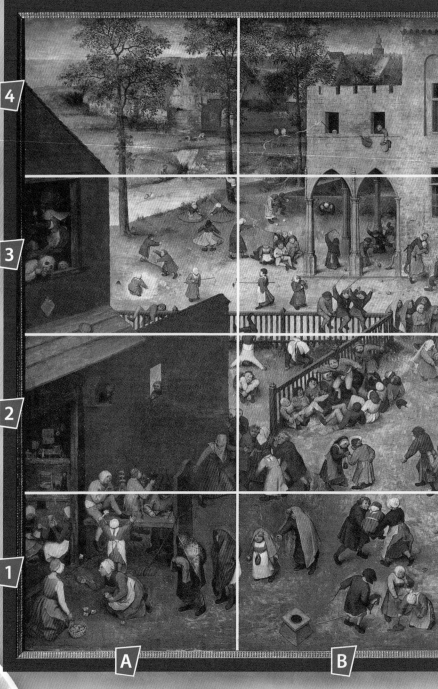

play leapfrog

play marbles

play with a top

dance

Children's Games
Pieter Brueghel
the elder

Children's games

1 Make a spinner.

Cut.

Glue the string.

Fold.

Spin.

C   D

2 Read and find.

1 He's riding a horse. He's in square B1.

2 She's playing with a ball. She's in D3.

3 He's climbing a tree. He's in A3.

4 He's swimming in the river. He's in A3.

1 **Listen and point.** 🔊 3.28 **Listen again and repeat.**

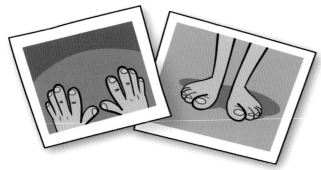

photo   fingers   feet

Dad   dance   dolphin   dinosaur

2 **Listen and find.** 🔊 3.29 **Point, ask and answer.**

What's he doing?

He's eating a sandwich.

What's she doing?

She's dancing.

Me and my world

1 Read and number.
2 Read again, listen and check. 3.31

2 I love dancing and music. We have a festival every year. We dance in the streets and play music too. In this photo, I'm wearing traditional Irish dress and I'm dancing with my friends.

I'm Sonya. I'm from Ireland. In this photo, my sister is playing the harp in a festival. The harp is a traditional Irish instrument. My friend Alex is playing the violin.

In this photo, I'm making a kite with my friends. Uttarayan is my favourite festival. It's in January.

My name's Nihar. I'm from India. I feel very happy on the day of Uttarayan, the kite festival. The sky is blue and you can see hundreds of kites. They are lots of different colours.

Revision

Play the game!

Start

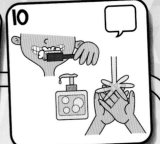

Finish

Christmas!

1 **Read and say** *True* **or** *False*.

1 It's got 5 stars.
2 It's got an angel.
3 It's got 6 snowflakes.
4 It's got 4 candles.
5 It's got 4 presents.
6 It's got 7 balls.
7 It's got 9 lights.
8 It's got 3 bells.

angel
star
snowflake
present
bell
candle
ball

2 **Listen and sing.** 3.33

1 Listen and say what colours. 3.34

2 Read and answer.

1 Is the yellow egg on the table?

2 Is the grey egg in the box?

3 Is the black egg under the flowerpot?

4 Is the brown and white egg on the flowers?

5 Is the blue and yellow egg under the tree?

6 Is the pink and white egg in the basket?

Tree Day

1 Listen and find. 🔘 3.35

a leaf

an apple tree

an oak tree

an orange tree

a palm tree

2 Look and answer.

What is it?

It's an apple leaf.

Songs and chants

Unit 1

Page 3
 1.2
Monday, Tuesday,
Wednesday, Thursday,
Friday, Saturday,
Sunday.

Page 7
1.10
Hello, what's your name?
Hello, come and play!
Hello, don't be shy!
Come and be my friend!

Let's run and jump and ride
  our bikes,
Kick a ball and fly our kites,
Watch TV and stay the night,
Come and be my friend!

Page 8
1.11
11, 12, 13, 14, 15
16, 17, 18, 19, 20
21, 22, 23, 24, 25
26, 27, 28, 29, 30

Unit 2

Page 11
1.18
Hey ho, this is my treehouse,
Hey ho, have a look and see!
I've got a bed and a table
  and a shelf and a cupboard,
A rug and a cushion and an
  old wooden chair.
Hey ho, this is my treehouse,
Hey ho, have a look and see!

Page 15
1.24
Big books, small books,
Books on the shelf!
Books are fun,
Books can help!

Books about animals,
Books about stars,
Books full of stories,
Books full of cars.

Books about children,
Books about birds,
Books full of pictures,
Books full of words.

Big books, small books,
Look on the shelf!
Books are fun,
Books can help!

Unit 3

Page 19
1.29
Come and play, come and play,
We've got lots of toys today.
Here's a skateboard, here's a bike,
Here's a frisbee, here's a kite.

Come and play, come and play,
We've got lots of toys today.
Here's a yo-yo, here's a ball,
Here's a skipping rope for you all.

Page 23   I like skipping,
 1.35   1, 2, 3!
I want Lucy
In with me!

Ride a scooter,
Ride a train,
Ride a bike,
Now spell your name!

L–U–C–Y

Goodbye, Lucy,
Wave at me!
Goodbye, Lucy,
1, 2, 3!

Unit 4

Page 29   Walk like a penguin,
2.2   Fly like a bat,
Run like a zebra,
Stretch like a cat,
Swim like a dolphin,
Slide like a snake,
Talk like a parrot,
Count to eight …
1, 2, 3, 4, 5, 6, 7, 8!

Page 33   The monkey says
2.10   'Now all watch me.'
The monkey says
'Look carefully.'
Can you do this?
Can you do this?
I can,
I can't,
And that's OK.
I can,
I can't,
We all can play!

Who's the monkey now?

Unit 5

Page 37   I want stickers,
 2.16   I want marbles,
I want balloons,
And key rings too.
I want dinosaurs,
I want badges,
I want felt tips,
What about you?

Page 41   Let's make a card for Mum.
 2.22   Yes, OK!
Let's make a card for Mum.
Yes, OK!
Let's make a card and say
'Hope you have a happy day'.
Let's make a card for Mum.
Yes, OK!

Let's make a cake for Grandma.
Yes, OK!
Let's make a cake for Grandma.
Yes, OK!
Let's make a cake and say
'Hope you have a happy day'.
Let's make a cake for Grandma.
Yes, OK!

Let's make a badge for Dad.
Yes, OK!
Let's make a badge for Dad.
Yes, OK!
Let's make a badge and say
'Hope you have a happy day'.
Let's make a badge for Dad.
Yes, OK!

Unit 6

Page 45 2.29

Welcome to the sandwich shop.
E-I-E-I-O.
Come and tell me what you want.
E-I-E-I-O.
I've got cheese and tuna,
I've got sardines too.
Chicken, tomato,
White bread, brown bread ...
Welcome to the sandwich shop,
E-I-E-I-O.

Page 49 2.36

Eggs and cheese for lunch today,
Ah-hum, Ah-hum.
Eggs and cheese for lunch today,
Ah-hum, Ah-hum.
Eggs and cheese for lunch today,
I'm trying something new today!
Ah-hum, Ah-hum, Ah-hum.

Can I have a little bit?
Ah-hum, Ah-hum.
Can I have a little bit?
Ah-hum, Ah-hum.
Can I have a little bit?
Look at me, I'm eating it!
Ah-hum, Ah-hum, Ah-hum.

Well, I like eggs and I like cheese,
Ah-hum, Ah-hum.
I like eggs and I like cheese,
Ah-hum, Ah-hum.
I like eggs and I like cheese.
Can I have some more now, please!
Ah-hum, Ah-hum, Ah-hum.

Unit 7

Page 55 2.45

If you're happy
Clap your hands!
If you're dizzy
Hold your head!
If you're cold
Swing your arms!
If you're sleepy
Go to bed!
If you're sad
Rub your eyes!
If you're cross
Stamp your feet!
If you're thirsty
Have a drink!
If you're hungry
Eat, eat, eat!

Page 59 2.52

Smile at me when I feel sad,
I feel sad,
I feel sad.
Smile at me when I feel sad,
Now I feel better.

Play with me when I feel bored,
I feel bored,
I feel bored.
Play with me when I feel bored,
Now I feel better.

Talk to me when I feel cross,
I feel cross,
I feel cross.
Talk to me when I feel cross,
Now I feel better.

Hold my hand when I feel scared,
I feel scared,
I feel scared.
Hold my hand when I feel scared,
Now I feel better.

Unit 8

Page 63 3.6

Paint a picture!
Read a book!
Play on the computer!
Help Mum cook!
Make a model!
Watch TV!
Do a puzzle!
Play with me!

___

Page 67 3.12

Oh, I'm lying on the sofa.
I'm sitting in the sun.
I'm bored of doing nothing.
Let's go out and have some fun!

Oh, I'm running in the garden.
I'm climbing up a tree.
I'm hungry and I'm thirsty.
Let's go and have our tea!

Oh, I'm painting lots of pictures.
I'm playing with my kite.
I'm sleepy and it's bedtime.
Let's go to bed – goodnight!

___

Unit 9

Page 71 3.19

I'm swimming.
Smile please!
I'm eating.
Smile please!
I'm writing.
Smile please!
Smile for your photo now, please.

I'm floating.
Smile please!
I'm reading.
Smile please!
I'm drinking.
Smile please!
Smile for your photo now, please.

Page 75 3.25

Summer's here,
Let's play in the sun.
We can swim, we can float,
We can jump, we can run.
But the sun is hot,
So remember the rules,
In the garden, at the beach and the
   swimming pool!

Wear a T-shirt,
Wear a hat,
Put cream on your face,
On your legs and your back.
Drink a lot of water,
Remember the rules,
In the garden, at the beach and the
   swimming pool!

___

Christmas

Page 81 3.33

Christmas Day is here again,
Lights shine in the streets.
Stars and bells and candles,
On our Christmas tree.

Christmas Day is here again,
Lights shine in the streets.
Happy Christmas, everyone.
Peace to you and me.

 **Let's practise!**

1 Listen and write the numbers. There is one example. 🔘 3.36

a [ ]

b [ ]

c [ ]

d [*1*]

e [ ]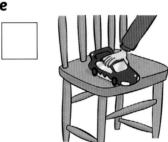

f [ ]

2 Listen and draw lines. There is one example. 🔘 3.37

1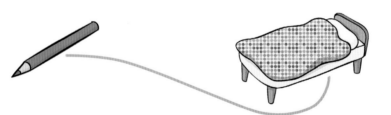

4

2

5

3

6

Starters Listening

Listen and draw lines. There is one example. 🔊 3.38

 **Let's practise!**

1 Read and colour. There is one example.

The ruler in the bag is grey.
The ruler on the chair is blue.
The sock on the table is purple.
The sock under the chair is pink.
The pen in the bag is green.
The pen under the table is red.

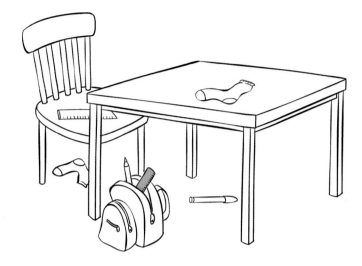

2 Look, read and draw lines. There is one example.

1	A man	**a**	has got a car.
2	The baby	**b**	has got a dress.
3	The woman	**c**	has got a hat.
4	A girl	**d**	has got a rabbit.
5	A boy	**e**	has got black legs.
6	The dog	**f**	has got two children.

Reading & Writing

Look and read. Write **yes** or **no**. There are two examples.

Examples

The man has got a white jacket.	.........**no**.........
The girl is in the car.	.........**yes**.........

Questions

1	The woman has got a green hat.	....
2	The kite in the tree is orange.	....
3	The big horse is brown.	....
4	A boy has got a ball.	....
5	The white duck is under the cow.	....

Starters Let's practise!

1 Listen and circle. There is one example. 🔊 3.39
Then ask and answer.

		Tony	Pam	Tom

1 What's your name?   Tony   Pam   (Tom)

2 How old are you?   7   8   9

3 What colour's your hair?

4 What are you wearing today?

5 What's your favourite food?

2 Listen and point to the people. 🔊 3.40 Then read and draw lines.
There is one example.

1 Who's eating an ice cream?   **a** They're climbing.
2 What's Kim's mum doing?   **b** On a chair.
3 What colour is Kim's dad's T-shirt?   **c** She's reading.
4 Where's Kim's grandpa sitting?   **d** A T-shirt and trousers.
5 What are Kim's brothers doing?   **e** Kim.
6 What's Kim's mum wearing?   **f** It's orange.

Starters Listening

Listen and put a tick (✔) in the box. There is one example. ◉ 3.41

What's Lucy's brother doing?

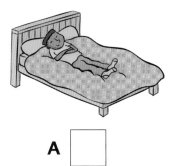 A ☐

 B ✔

 C ☐

1 Where's Nick's ball?

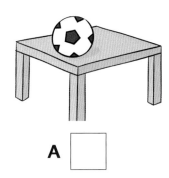 A ☐

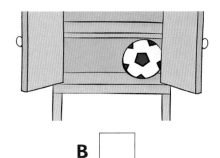 B ☐

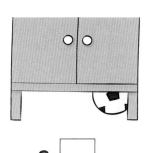 C ☐

2 What's Anna wearing?

 A ☐

 B ☐

 C ☐

3 Where's Ben's mum?

 A ☐

 B ☐

 C ☐

Let's practise!

1 Look at the pictures and read the questions.
Circle the answers. There are two examples.

Examples

What's the boy eating?
(a banana) / a sandwich / a cake

How many ice creams has the man got?
two / three / (four)

Questions

1 Where's the woman sitting?
on a rug / on a chair / on a table

2 Who's wearing a hat?
the man / the woman / the girl

3 How many children are in the water?
one / two / three

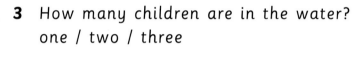

4 What's the girl got?
a frisbee / a balloon / a ball

5 What's the dog doing now?
running / swimming / sleeping

Starters Reading & Writing

Look at the pictures and read the questions.
Write one-word answers. There are two examples.

Examples

What colour are the cars?   ___**red**___

Who's got a crocodile?   the ___**boy**___

Questions

1   What's the girl drawing?   a _____

2   How many books are on the table now?
    _____

3   What's the girl doing now?   _____

4   Where's the crocodile now?
    under the _____

5   What's the boy doing? _____

ACKNOWLEDGEMENTS

Main illustrations by: Gustavo Mazali

Other illustrations by: Aardvart p.44 (bottom); Kathy Baxendale p.27; Beccy Blake
pp.7, 15, 23, 33, 41, 49, 59, 67, 75; Judy Brown pp.88, 89, 90, 91, 92, 93, 94, 95;
Christiane Engel/Thorogood pp.34, 35; John Haslam pp.28, 54, 80; Dusan Pavlic/
Beehive Illustration pp.6 (top), 32; Andres Martinez Ricci/The Organisation
pp.10, 18, 26, 36, 44 (top), 52, 62 (top). 70, 78; Simon Smith p.74.

Cover by: Gustavo Mazali.

Commissioned photography by: Gareth Boden all make and do photography pp.9,
17, 25, 35, 43, 51, 61, 69, 77; Phil James pp.34–35 (pencils); MM Studios pp.8, 9,
42, 43, 51 (meals).

*The Publishers would also like to thank the following for their kind permission to reproduce
photographs and other copyright material*: Alamy pp.27 (boys/Robert Landau),
36 (rabbit/PetStockBoys, crocodile/Steve Allen Travel Photography, zebra/Michael
Diggin, duck/William Leaman), 50 (sardines/Foodfolio, bread/Graham Kirk/The
Anthony Blake Picture Library), 52 (eggs/Sue Wilson, carrots/WoodyStock,
chocolate/Keith Leighton, apples/Profimedia International s.r.o.), 53 (nasi lemak/
Simon Reddy, rice and milk/Bon Appetit), 70 (riding a bike/T.M.O. Pictures,
hopping/Chuck Franklin, washing up/Van hilversum), 78 (playing with doll/M
L Pearson), 79 (Irish band/Stephen Power, kite festival/Travel India, making
kites/Pep Roig); The Bridgeman Art Library pp.16 (Van Gogh's *Bedroom at Arles*,
1889 (oil on canvas), Gogh, Vincent van (1853–90)/Musee d'Orsay, Paris, France/
Giraudon; *Room in Brooklyn*, 1932 (oil on canvas), Hopper, Edward (1882–1967)/
Museum of Fine Arts, Boston, Massachusetts, USA/The Hayden Collection –
Charles Henry Hayden Fund), 17 (*Model with Unfinished Self Portrait*, 1977 (oil on
canvas), Hockney, David (b.1937)/Private Collection 60 x 60 © David Hockney),
76–77 (*Children's Games* (*Kinderspiele*), 1560 (oil on panel), Bruegel, Pieter the
Elder (c.1525–69)/Kunsthistorisches Museum, Vienna, Austria); Corbis
p.53 (blinis/B. Marielle/photocuisine), 78 (dancing/Anna Peisl, horse riding/
Nugene Chiang/Mind Body Soul), 79 (Irish dancing/Barry Lewis/InPictures);
Getty Images pp.24 (helicopters/Steve Gorton/Dorling Kindersley, bikes/Andy
Crawford/Dorling Kindersley, motorbike/CSA Plastock, lorries/David Arky,
blue car/Konrad Zelakowski, van/Tim Ridley), 25 (helicopter/Steve Gorton/
Dorling Kindersley, bikes/Andy Crawford/Dorling Kindersley, motorbike/CSA
Plastock, blue car/Konrad Zelakowski), 36 (lion/Heinrich van den Berg/Gallo
Images, dolphin/Andy Rouse/StockImage), 50 (sausages/Patrice De Villiers/Stone,
pasta/Jan Cobb Photography Ltd, Photographer's Choice, rice/Dorling Kindersley,
yoghurt/Andy Crawford/Dorling Kindersley, cheese/Dorling Kindersley, lettuce/
Eisenhut and Mayer Wien/Foodpix), 52 (cheese/Dorling Kindersley, sardines/
Dorling Kindersley), 68 (shower/Roger Charity/Photonica, teeth/Peter Cade/
Iconica), 69 (bath/Peter Dazeley/Phoyographer's Choice, washing hands/Steven
Puetzer/Photonica), 70 (cooking/Dave King/Dorling Kindersley, cleaning teeth/
DAJ/amana images, painting/Bill Losh/Taxi, sleeping/Susan Barr/Workbook
Stock), 78 (eating/Bipolar, reading/Vanessa Davies/Dorling Kindersley, swimming/
Laurence Monneret/StockImage, taking a photo/Jessie Jean/The Image Bank,
watching tv/Donna Day/Stone); Oxford University Press pp.18, 24 (plane, boat,
red car), 25 (red car), 27 (girls), 36 (monkey, snake), 50 (apple, banana, orange,
carrots), 52 (sausages, lettuce, rice, yoghurt, bananas, milk), 53 (girl, boy, flour,
milk and eggs), 60 (musical instruments), 68 (washing up), 70 (frisbee);
Photolibrary p.50 (tuna/Geoff Langan/Anthony Blake Photo Library, chicken/
Tim Ridley); Royal Mint pp.42, 43 (coins).